PHOTOGRAPHY;

INCLUDING THE

DAGUERREOTYPE, CALOTYPE, CHRYSOTYPE, &c.

FAMILIARLY EXPLAINED;

BEING

A Treatise on its Objects and Uses,

AND ON THE

METHODS OF PREPARING SENSITIVE PAPER, METALLIC PLATES, ETC., FOR TAKING PICTURES BY THE AGENCY OF LIGHT.

BY

W. RALEIGH BAXTER, M.R.C.S.,

Licentiate of Apothecaries' Hall, Dublin and London; late Lecturer on Natural History in the Peter-street School of Medicine, Dublin; Lecturer on Materia Medica in the Charlotte-street School of Medicine, London; Lecturer on Physiology in the Royal Polytechnic Institution of London; Author of Bentley's Hand-Book of Chemistry, &c.

[Second Edition.]

LONDON:

HENRY RENSHAW, 356, STRAND.

1842.

The Compiler takes leave to express his thanks to the Editors of various Newspapers and Periodicals for the high complimentary notices they were pleased to bestow on the First Edition of this Work.

PHOTOGRAPHY, &c.

THE art of Photography is one of the most pleasing and curious results of chemical philosophy, and certainly not one of the least useful. Those who have beheld on the field of a camera obscura the minutely perfect reflection of a landscape, with its rivulet, its well-clad trees, and its animated groups, must have regretted that it was but a shadow doomed to exist only for a moment, while the light shone or the instrument remained stationary. Photography, however, enables us to render permanent the objects thus reflected. To accomplish this, no tedious or troublesome process is necessary; unlike the creations of the artist's pencil, the pictures thus produced are not the result of long and tiring manipulation. In a moment our work is over—our desires accomplished.

In order that the reader, who may have hitherto paid but little attention to such subjects, may form some idea of the mode in which light acts so as to produce pictures upon prepared paper or metallic plates, rendered sensitive to its influence, we shall for a short time refer to certain well-known effects of light on plants, animals, and chemical compounds.

Light is the cause of colour in plants, in animals, and in minerals. The ruby, the humming-bird, and the violet, are enriched from the same source. We shall endeavour to explain this in a familiar manner. A ray of light, although perfectly white to the eye, consists, in fact, of "a bundle of rays," of different colours, and possessed of different functions, while on the absorption or reflection of the various rays depends the varieties of all coloured bodies. It is to Sir Isaac Newton that we owe this discovery. The instrument employed for the purpose of decomposing a ray of light is a triangular piece of glass called a *prism*, and the party-coloured figure produced by its agency is called the *prismatic spectrum*. The effect produced by means of the prism is owing to the different refrangibility of the seven coloured rays of light. The *violet* ray suffers the greatest refraction, and is therefore found at the top of the *spectrum*, while the *red*, being least refrangible, is found at the bottom. The other rays are disposed according to their different degrees of refrangibility. If the spectrum be divided into 360 equal parts, to correspond with the 360 degrees of the circle, the *violet* colour will be found to occupy 80 of the parts, the *indigo* 40, the *blue* 60, the *green* 60, the *yellow* 48, the *orange* 27, and the *red* 45.

We may remark here, that Sir David Brewster has proved that the term primary colours, applied to the seven coloured rays in the spectrum, is incorrect, as there are in reality only *three* primary ones, *blue*, *yellow*, and *red*, while all the others are merely modifications of them.

When bodies reflect or turn back all the rays of light which fall upon them, they are termed *white;* but, on the contrary, when all the rays are absorbed, we call the bodies thus absorbing the light, *black*, indicating, in fact, a total absence of colour. Thus, again, every substance in nature will appear of that particular colour of the spectrum which its construction will enable it to reflect. Thus, for example, the colour called *blue*, or *red*, is produced in bodies by an absorption of all the other rays except the *blue* or *red*, which are reflected, and therefore become visible to the eye.

However, colour is not the only property which light bestows even upon plants. Taste, odour, and combustibility, are derived from the same source; and " the spicy gums of Araby," the medicinal plants of Southern America, and the odoriferous resins of the East, owe their qualities to the abundance of light falling upon their native soils. Such, too, is the influence of light upon the organism of plants, that in sunlight they pour forth streams of vital air, or oxygen, while in the shade, on the contrary, they exhale poisonous carbonic acid.

If a plant bearing flowers be placed near a window, the flowers will all seek the light, approximating as nearly as possible to the window. Those flowers, too, which bloom on the side nearest the window are always of a more beautiful colour and healthful appearance than those more remote from the light. Again, if a plant, hitherto bearing beautiful flowers and green leaves, were transported to a spot to which light had no access whatever, it would not only become sickly, but would actually in time be rendered colourless, and so altered in appearance as no longer to present the distinguishing features of the family to which it belonged. There are many cases on record where the seeds and roots of well-known plants have accidentally found their way into dark mines and coal-pits, and have there vegetated, but so altered have the products been, owing to the absence of light, that even botanists have failed to recognise their species. The outside of many of our esculent vegetables is beautifully green, while the heart is colourless; for instance, the cabbage and the lettuce. The colour of the outside is owing to the influence of light; the whiteness of the heart is owing to its absence. Market gardeners are well aware of these facts, and in order to preserve these vegetables white and tender, they are covered as much as possible from light during their growth. This operation is termed " bleaching;" in the cabbage and lettuce it is produced by tying the leaves of the plants together; in celery it is produced by covering as much of the vegetable as possible by means of earth.

Light has a great effect upon the health and appearance of animals as well as of plants. This is very apparent in the poor creatures who toil in our coal-mines; and the squalor and dwarfishness to be seen in the narrow courts of large cities may be traced as much to the absence of light as to the imperfect ventilation of these place and the insufficiency of food. The animals found in the polar regions are almost destitute of colour, being merely of a dingy whiteness; but the reverse obtains among the inhabitants of the tropics. There the birds have a plumage rich and varied in colour; indeed, the animal and vegetable productions of those countries where light and heat are most abundant, are more numerous, precocious, and extensive in their dimensions. We must not omit to mention the different effects of light upon the colours of the living and of the dead plant. That very agency which gave to the leaf or flower its richness of hue during life, the moment it has ceased to exist, actually becomes a bleaching agent, and robs it of its beautiful tints. Most of the colours employed for dyeing are of vegetable origin and every housewife knows what havoc sunlight makes upon her papered rooms, her curtains, and her carpets. Even such of the precious gems as owe their value to the richness of their colours are injured by exposure to light; the ancients noticed this fact especially in connection with the opal and the amethyst.

Having noticed the action of light upon plants and animals, we shall consider some of its effects upon certain chemical combinations. Here, however, the field that opens upon us is so extensive, that our principal difficulty will be how to choose from so large a number of examples these which are most striking. "There is not a substance," remarks Fourcroy, "which in well-closed glass vessels, and exposed to the sun's light, does not experience some alteration from this cause. Among these, the mineral acids, the metallic oxides or calces, vegetable powders, and volatile animal oils, are most singularly changed. Metallic oxides in general, especially those of mercury, become of a deeper colour by exposure to the sun; as may be seen by observing painters' colours which are preserved in powder in the shops. The mineral acids by the same treatment become higher coloured, more volatile and fuming. Metallic salts grow black, and animal oils take an obscure brown." Many of these effects of light were first noticed by the celebrated Scheele, and next by Berthollet.

However, the first parties who noticed the effect of the sun's rays upon metallic compounds were the alchemists. They were in the habit of filling a bottle with a salt now called the chloride of silver, but called then *luna cornea*, or horn silver, a compound exceedingly sensitive to light, and after cutting out certain devices upon black paper, it was laid upon the bottle, and the whole exposed to the light. Where the sun's rays had had access to the compound, the salt was blackened, while the portions protected by the paper remained white. But although the alchemists had by this experiment actually stumbled upon the threshold of the discovery of Photography, yet so intent were they upon their absurd search after the philosopher's stone, that every thing which did not promise them the desired result was thrown aside as useless.

The first person who seems to have had any notion of Photography was Mr. Wedgwood, whose mind was led to the subject by observing that light blackened a solution of nitrate of silver, or lunar caustic. If any of our readers have had at any time occasion to employ this salt, they no doubt have noticed that paper, or linen, or the skin, if touched with it, in a short time becomes black. This is owing to the action of light; for if the objects thus touched were kept in the dark, no change would be perceptible. It is on this account that marking ink becomes gradually blacker. The principal ingredient in that preparation is nitrate of silver, and being a sensitive compound, is acted upon by the light. A knowledge of these facts led Mr. Wedgwood to perform his first experiment, which was thus conducted :—

He took a solution of nitrate of silver, and having covered a piece of writing paper with it, exposed it behind a painting on glass to the sun's rays. Of course, wherever the rays of light could fall upon the paper, it blackened; the portion protected remained white. Now, could he have arrested the further influence of light, and thus have fixed the picture, he would have accomplished nearly all that was necessary—as in our day the employment of a more sensitive compound than nitrate of silver gives a difference in degree, and not in principle. But although Mr. Wedgwood, together with Sir Humphrey Davy, experimented carefully, the object of fixation could not be accomplished, and the whole ended in failure.

In the first volume of the " Journal of the Royal Institution," published in 1802, there is a short memoir on the subject, by Sir Humphrey Davy. In this memoir the talented writer gives Mr. Wedgwood the credit of having originated the first notion of the art. The following record of the failure of these two great men is extracted from the memoir just quoted :—" The copy of a painting, immediately after being taken, must be kept in an obscure place. It may indeed be examined in the shade, but even in this case the exposure should be only for a few minutes. *No attempts that have been made to fix the pictures have as yet been successful.* They have been covered with a thin coating of fine varnish, but this has not preserved them. The images formed by means of a camera obscura have been found to be too faint to produce an effect upon the nitrate of silver in any moderate time. To copy these images was the first object of Mr. Wedgwood, but all his numerous experiments proved unsuccessful."

About this time the scientific world was busily engaged in ascertaining the existence and locality of the chemical rays of light. It was discovered by M. Ritter and Dr. Wollaston, that if the muriate of silver were exposed in a spectrum to the least refrangible rays, or those which give the greatest amount of heat without light, no effect was produced upon it; but when exposed to the most refrangible ray, the *violet*, it was rapidly blackened, and even beyond the *violet* ray, in a space perfectly invisible to our eyes, the darkening effect was most apparent. Thus, as there are invisible rays beyond the *red*, giving heat without light, so are there beyond the *violet* ray others which, although beyond the range of vision, have the maximum intensity of chemical action. These interesting researches were verified by Berard, Lubeck, and Berthollet, Sir William Herschel, Sir Henry Englefield, Sir Humphrey Davy, and others; nor should we omit to mention the experiments of our countrywoman, Mrs. Mary Somerville, who demonstrated that a needle might be magnetized by exposing it to the *violet* ray—a fact originally announced by Professor Morichini, of Rome, verified by Professor Configliachi, at Pavia, and by M. Berard, at Montpellier.

It was at one time supposed that terrestrial or artificial light possessed no chemical rays, but this is incorrect. Mr. Brande found that although the concentrated light of the moon, or the light even of olefiant gas, however intense, had no effect on chloride of silver, or on a mixture of chlorine and hydrogen, yet the light emitted by electrized charcoal blackens the salt, and explodes the gases. At the Royal Polytechnic Institution pictures have been taken by means of sensitive paper acted upon by the Drummond light. The longest time required was 30 seconds, and the paper was sensibly darkened in one second. Nor was there any attempt made in this case to concentrate the rays; no reflector being used.

After the failure of such men as Wedgwood and Davy, it is not to be wondered at that the subject should have been dropped. In fact, nothing more was heard of it for thirty years, although during a portion of that time, both here and abroad, several persons had resumed for investigation.

It appears that M. Niepse, of Chalons on the Soane, commenced his researches in 1814. His early attempts seem to have been marked with but small success, for he pursued his experiments alone for ten years. He then became acquainted with M. Daguerre, who was at that time busily engaged in a kindred pursuit, and in 1839 the process termed Daguerreotype was published to the world. However, six months before the French philosophers had published their discoveries, Mr. Fox Talbot had communicated to the Royal Society *his* method of rendering paper sensitive, as well as his mode of fixation. Thus both in France and England, at one and the same time, unknown to each other, Talbot and Daguerre were pursuing the same object, and each with signal success. Since then Mr. Talbot has assiduously followed up his first discovery, by repeated experiments, and the result is the modification of the process, termed the Calotype, from the Greek words signifying " beautiful picture or image."

Mr. Talbot's first sensitive paper was prepared as follows :— Take superfine writing paper, dip it in a weak solution of common salt (about half an ounce to the pint of water), and wipe it dry, by which the salt is uniformly distributed throughout its surface. Then spread a solution of nitrate of silver (twenty grains of the nitrate to an ounce of water) on one side, and dry it at the fire, and the paper is ready to receive an image. When a picture was produced, it was rendered insensible to light by washing it over with a weak solution of iodide of potassium, and then in distilled water. Mr. Talbot produced a still more sensitive paper by substituting a solution of bromide of potassium for the common salt in the above process.

THE DAGUERREOTYPE.

The process of M. Daguerre is as follows :—Having obtained plates of copper plated with silver (the copper being of a sufficient thickness to insure the silver surface from warping, which would distort the image when obtained), the first and most important part of the operation is rendering the silver side of the plate as clean as possible, because if there is the least speck of dirt on any part of the plate, that part is not acted upon in the future processes, thus causing a corresponding defect in the picture. The plate is first rubbed over with a mixture of finely powdered Tripoli, or pumice stone mixed with oil; this preparation is applied by means of a small piece of cotton wool, after having been rubbed for some time with the above mixture, it is rubbed with dry Tripoli, which imparts to it a fine polish, but this is not enough. It is now to be washed over with dilute nitric acid, and when quite cleared from that by means of distilled water, is to be again rubbed over with the Tripoli and oil, and dry Tripoli, and when the plate is used it is rubbed with lampblack sifted on a piece of velvet, which is tightly strained over a flat surface of wood, forming an instrument termed technically " a buff," which is generally in the form of a large razor-strop. When the plate has acquired a golden yellow colour, it is removed from the box, and is ready to receive an image. It is then placed in the camera, and after remaining there a time, varying from two minutes to a quarter of an hour (according to the intensity of the light), it is removed, but no trace of the picture is visible. In order to develop it, it is placed in another box, containing mercury, which is heated to about 140° of Fahrenheit, in order to volatilize it. In a few minutes the picture begins to appear, the mercury attaching itself to those parts which have been acted on by the light, and the picture becomes visible. Those parts of the picture which have been most exposed to light receive the largest quantity of mercury, thus producing the strongest light, and *vice versâ*. In order to fix the picture, it is washed in hot distilled water, then in a solution of hyposulphite of soda, then again in distilled water, and the operation is finished. This process, besides having the advantage of rendering the plates more sensitive to light than Mr. Talbot's paper, was possessed of another and a very decisive preference, for the picture produced by it had the lights and shades in their proper position, which Mr. Talbot's pictures had not. Since the first introduction of this process it has been very much improved upon. Compounds have been discovered which have rendered the plates much more sensitive than the plain iodine. Instead of the time above mentioned for taking the picture being required, we can now produce the requisite effect in favourable weather in half a second. The compounds of iodine with chlorine, and of bromine with chlorine, are now employed, and are known under the names of chloride of iodine and chloride of bromine.

Some time after this Dr. Schafhœntl introduced to the notice of the British Association a new method of Photographic drawing, but it is so complex and difficult of execution, that it would be next to useless to describe it.

THE CALOTYPE.

The Calotype differs very materially from the earlier Photographic processes in many points. We shall now proceed to enumerate a few of the most prominent. The image formed upon the Calotype paper is at first invisible; for although the object has been reflected on the paper in the camera, or even has been in contact with it, yet on removing it from the light no trace can be perceived. This certainly is the most mysterious part of the process, and one which arrests almost more than any other the attention of the manipulator. The paper prepared by this process is also vastly more sensitive; however, this is a difference rather of degree than of kind. The fixation of the pictures is also so much superior, that it admits of a great number of copies being taken from each camera picture, which could not be done by the former method, at least not with any certainty.

In taking an image in the camera by the common Calotype process, the first impression is always a negative one. By a negative picture we mean one in which the lights and shadows are reversed, giving the whole an appearance not conformable to nature. For instance, if we were to copy a piece of black lace, we should have in the first case white lace upon a dark ground; but upon taking a second copy, upon sensitive paper, we should then have what is termed a positive image, conformable to the original—viz, black lace upon a white ground. In sitting for a portrait, the same result would take place if the common Calotype mode were employed; and although Mr. Talbot has pointed out a method of taking positive pictures at once, yet, as it is somewhat complicated and difficult, we would strongly recommend the experimenter to take images by the common mode first, and then recopy them upon sensitive paper.

In order to obtain a positive copy, it is best not to employ the Calotype paper, as it is too sensitive. The common Photographic paper, prepared as follows, will answer the purpose more completely:—

Dissolve 25 grains of chloride of sodium (common salt) in one ounce of distilled water; soak the paper in it some time, and then dry between blotting paper. Next dissolve 90 grains of crystallized nitrate of silver in an ounce of distilled water, and brush the paper with it twice, drying it by a fire between each washing. Keep it in the dark until wanted for use. Before taking the positive copy, cover the paper containing the negative image with white wax, to render it transparent, so that the light may pass more readily through it. This may be done by scraping the wax upon the paper, and then, after placing it between two other portions of paper, passing a heated iron over it.

Preparation of the Calotype Paper.

In describing the mode of rendering paper sensitive, we adopt Mr. Talbot's directions.

First Part of the Preparation of the Paper.

Mr Talbot dissolves 100 grains of crystallized nitrate of silver in six ounces of distilled water; washes one side of the paper with this solution with a soft camel-hair brush, and places a mark upon that side by which to know it again; he dries the paper cautiously at a distant fire, or else leaves it to dry spontaneously in a dark place. Next he dips the paper in a solution of iodide of potassium, containing 500 grains of that salt dissolved in one pint of water, and leaves the paper a minute or two in this solution; then takes it out and dips it in water; then dries it lightly with blotting paper, and finishes by drying at a fire, or else leaves it to dry spontaneously. All this process is best done in the evening by candle light. The paper thus far prepared may be called, for the sake of distinction, iodized paper. This iodized paper is scarcely sensitive to light, but nevertheless it should be kept in a portfolio or some dark place till wanted for use. It does not spoil by keeping any length of time, provided it is not exposed to light.

Second Part of the Preparation of the Paper.

This second part is best deferred until the paper is wanted for use. When that time is arrived, Mr. Talbot takes a sheet of the iodized paper and washes it with a liquid prepared in the following manner:—Dissolve 100 grains of crystallized nitrate of silver in two ounces of distilled water; to this solution add one-sixth of its volume of strong acetic acid; let this mixture be called A; dissolve crystallized gallic acid in distilled water, as much as it will dissolve (which is a very small quantity); let this solution be called B. When you wish to prepare a sheet of paper for use, mix together the liquids, A and B, in equal volumes This mixture is called by the name of gallo-nitrate of silver. Let no more be mixed than is intended to be used at one time, because the mixture will not keep good for a long period. Then take a sheet of iodized paper and wash it over with this gallo-nitrate of silver with a soft camel hair-brush, taking care to wash it on the side which has been previously marked. This operation should be performed by candle-light. Let the paper rest half a minute, and then dip it into water, and dry it lightly with blotting paper; and, lastly, dry it cautiously at a fire, holding it at a considerable distance therefrom. When dry, the paper is fit for use; but it is advisable to use it within a few hours after its preparation. If it is so used immediately, the last drying may be dispensed with, and the paper may be used moist.

Instead of using a solution of gallic acid for the liquid B, the tincture of galls diluted with water may be used, but it is not so advisable.

Use of the Paper.

The paper thus prepared, and which has been named Calotype paper, is placed in a camera obscura, so as to receive the image formed in the focus of the lens. Of course the paper must be screened or defended from the light during the time it is being put into the camera. When the camera is properly pointed at the object, this screen is withdrawn, or a pair of internal folding doors are opened, so as to expose the paper for the reception of the image. If the object is very bright, or the time is short, or the objects dim, no image whatever is visible upon the paper, which appears entirely blank. Nevertheless, it is impressed with an invisible image, and the means of causing this image to become visible have been discovered. This is performed as follows:—Take some gallo-nitrate of silver, prepared in the manner before directed, and with this liquid wash the paper all over with a soft camel-hair brush. Then hold it before a gentle fire, and in a short time (varying from a few seconds to a minute or two) the image begins to appear upon the paper. Those parts of the paper upon which light has acted the most strongly become brown or black, while those parts on which light has not acted remain white. The image continues to strengthen and grow more and more visible during some time; when it appears strong enough, the operation should be determined and the picture fixed.

The Fixing Process.

In order to fix the picture thus obtained, first dip it into water, then partly dry it with blotting paper, and then wash it with a solution of bromide of potassium, containing 100 grains of the salt dissolved in eight or ten ounces of water. The picture is then washed with water, and then finally dried. Instead of bromide of potassium, a strong solution of common salt may be used, but it is less advisable. The picture thus obtained will have its lights and shades reversed. With respect to the natural objects—viz., the lights of the objects are represented by shades, and *vice versâ*. But it is easy from this picture to obtain another, which shall be conformable to nature—viz., in which the lights shall be represented by lights, and the shades by shades. It is only necessary for this purpose to take a second sheet of sensitive Calotype paper, and place it in close contact with the first, upon which the picture has been formed. A board is put beneath them, and a sheet of glass above, and the whole is pressed into close contact by screws. Being then exposed to day-light for a short time, an image or copy is formed upon the second sheet of paper. This image or copy is often invisible at first, but the image may be made to appear in the same way that has been already stated. But Mr. Talbot does not recommend that the copy should be taken on Calotype paper; on the contrary, he would advise that it should be taken on common Photographic paper. Although it takes a much longer time to obtain a copy upon this paper than upon Calotype paper, yet the tints of the copy are generally more harmonious and agreeable. On whatever paper the copy is taken it should be fixed in the way already described. After a Calotype picture has furnished a good many copies it sometimes grows faint, and the subsequent copies are inferior. This may be prevented by means of a process, which revives the strength of the Calotype pictures. In order to effect this it is only necessary to wash them by candle-light with gallo-nitrate of silver, and then warm them. This causes all the shades of the picture to darken considerably, while the white parts are not affected. After this the picture is of course to be fixed a second time. The picture will then yield a second series of copies, and a great number of them may frequently be made.

In the same way that a faded Calotype picture may be revived and restored, it is possible to strengthen and revive Photographs which have been made on other descriptions of sensitive paper; but these are inferior in beauty, and moreover the result is less to be depended on.

The next part of Mr. Talbot's invention consists in a mode of obtaining positive Photographic pictures, that is to say, Photographics, in which the lights of the object are represented by lights, and the shades by shades. How this may be done by a double process has already been described; but we shall now describe the means of doing it by a single process. Take a sheet of sensitive Calotype paper and expose it to day-light, until a slight but visible discoloration or browning of its surface is perceived; this generally occurs in a few seconds; then dip the paper into a solution of iodide of potassium, of the same strength as before; viz., 500 grains to one pint of water. This immersion apparently removes the visible impression caused by the light—nevertheless, it does not really remove it; for if the paper were to be now washed with gallo-nitrate of silver, it would speedily blacken all over. The paper, when taken out of the iodide of potassium, is dipped in water, and then lightly dried with blotting-paper. It is then placed in the focus of a camera obscura, which is pointed at an object. After five or ten minutes the paper is withdrawn and washed with gallo-nitrate of silver, and warmed as before directed. An image will then appear of a positive kind; namely, representing the lights of the object by lights, and the shades by shades. Engravings may be very well copied in the same way, and positive copies of them obtained at once (reversed, however, from right to left). For this purpose a sheet of Calotype paper is taken, and held in day-light to darken it, as before mentioned; but for the present purpose it should be more darkened that if it were intended to be used in the camera obscura. The rest of the process is the same. The engraving and the sensitive paper should be pressed into close contact, with screws or otherwise, and placed in the sunshine, which generally effects the copy in a minute or two. This copy, if it is not sufficiently distinct, must be rendered visible, or strengthened, with the gallo-nitrate of silver, as before described. "I am aware," says Mr. Talbot, "that the use of iodide of potassium for obtaining positive Photographs has been recommended by others; and I do not claim it by itself as a new invention, but only when used in conjunction with the gallo-nitrate of silver; or, when the pictures obtained are rendered visible or strengthened subsequently to their first formation. In order to take portraits from the life, I prefer to use for the object-glass of the camera, a lens, whose focal length is only three or four times greater than the diameter of the aperture. The person whose portrait is to be taken should be so placed that the head may be as steady as possible, and the camera being then pointed at it, an image is received on the sensitive Calotype paper. I prefer to conduct the process in the open air, under a serene sky, but without sunshine; the image is generally obtained in half a minute, or a minute. If sunshine is employed, a sheet of blue glass should be used as a screen to defend the eyes from too much glare, because this glass does not materially weaken the power of the chemical rays to affect the paper. The portrait thus obtained on the Calotype paper is a negative one; and from this a positive copy may be obtained in the way already described."

Mr. Talbot claims, first, the employing gallic-acid, or tincture of galls, in conjunction with a solution of silver, to render paper, which has received a previous preparation, more sensitive to the action of light; secondly, the making visible Photographic images upon paper, and the strengthening such images when already faintly or imperfectly visible, by washing them with liquids which have been previously acted upon by light; thirdly, the obtaining portraits from the life by Photographic means upon paper; fourthly, the employing bromide of potassium, or some other soluble bromide, for fixing the images obtained.

Dr. Ryan, the able professor of chemistry in the Polytechnic Institution, to whom the compiler of these sheets cannot too strongly express his gratitude for the kind assistance afforded him, has noticed that in the iodizing process the sensitiveness of the paper is materially injured by keeping it *too long* in the solution of iodide of potassium, owing to the newly formed iodide of silver being so exceedingly soluble in the excess of iodide of potassium as in a few minutes to be completely removed. The paper then should be merely dipped in the solution, and instantly removed.

There is another point, too, in the preparation of the iodized paper, in which Mr. Mitchell, Dr. Ryan's talented assistant, who has paid great attention to this branch of science, and zealously aided the writer in his investigations, suggests a slight deviation from Mr. Talbot's method. In the first instance he recommends the paper to be brushed over with the solution of the iodide of potassium, instead of the nitrate of silver—transposing, in fact, the application of the two first solutions. The paper having been brushed over with the iodide of potassium solution, is dried. It is then brushed over with nitrate of silver in solution, and after drying is dipped for a moment in the solution of iodide of potassium *—is again washed in distilled water and dried. By this means Mr. Mitchell states that he obtains a more sensitive paper, and a more even distribution of the compounds over the surface.

Dr. Ryan, at the Royal Polytechnic Institution, has been enabled to employ the strong glare of the Drummond light

* This solution is one fourth the strength of the original one recommended by Mr. Talbot.

during the preparation of the paper without any injury accruing, merely by covering the flame with a lanthorn of yellow glass, although without such a medium the paper would be completely spoiled in half a second. As in the preparation of the paper, both in the first and latter stages, it will be necessary to have a little light—a shade of yellow glass must be provided, which must be placed around the lamp or candle. Light passing through such a medium will scarcely affect the sensitive compounds, the yellow glass intercepting the chemical rays.

Apparatus to be Employed.

After carefully preparing the various solutions according to Mr. Talbot's plan, the following apparatus will be requisite :—

Two large shallow dishes to hold distilled water. We require *two*, as we must not wash the sensitive paper in the same water as that in which the fixed paper is to be placed. The water in which the sensitive paper is washed will frequently require changing, owing to the decomposition of the gallo-nitrate of silver.

Several large camel-hair or *badger brushes*, without any metal in contact with them. Each solution requires its distinct brush, which after use must be immediately washed in distilled water. The one employed for the gallo-nitrate is soon spoiled.

A graduated ounce measure, in which to place the equal proportions of solutions, A and B.

A large glass vessel, holding half a pint, for the solution of bromide of potassium.

A quantity of white bibulous paper, cut to the size, or nearly so, of the sensitive paper; in each stage of preparation distinct portions of bibulous paper must be used. If these be kept separate and marked they can be again used for the same purpose; but it would not do to dry the finished picture, for instance, in the same folds in which the sensitive paper had been dried.

A camera obscura, to take reflected objects. This may be obtained for a very small sum from any optician.

A couple of wooden frames with glass panels, and with hinges so as to press the object to be copied (lace for instance) into close contact with the sensitive paper. This apparatus may be used for taking a positive picture from a negative copy.

A tin or pewter vessel, to hold hot water, upon which the

paper is to be laid after receiving the second coating of gallo-nitrate. The water in the vessel should nearly boil.

A spirit lamp, in which naptha may be used.

A shade of yellow glass, to place between the light of the lamp or candle, in which case the preparation of the paper in total darkness is unnecessary.

After the introduction of the Calotype process by Mr. Talbot, a new method of taking pictures by light was introduced by Mr. Hunt. His method was as follows :—Highly glazed letter paper was washed over with a solution of one drachm of nitrate of silver to an ounce of distilled water; it is quickly dried, and a second time washed over with the same solution. It is then placed for a minute in a solution of one drachm of iodide of potassium in six ounces of water, and, being placed on a smooth board, gently washed by allowing pure water to flow over it; it is dried in the dark at common temperature. Papers thus prepared may be kept for any length of time, and are at any moment rendered far more sensitive than any known Photographic preparation except the Calotype, to which it is quite equal, by simply washing it over with a solution formed of one drachm of the ferrocyanide of potassium in an ounce of distilled water. These papers may be washed with the ferrocyanide and dried in the dark, and in this dry state they are absolutely insensible; but they may at any moment be rendered sensitive by merely washing with cold water. The paper is rendered quite insensible by being washed over with the above solution; and from the Photograph thus fixed many copies may be taken.

Although this art has been brought to the present state of perfection, it seems to be more the result of chance experimenting than inductive reasoning; for who could suppose that a plate of metal, on which no image was perceptible, would have had a picture developed by the vapour of mercury acting upon it ?—or in the case of the Calotype process, that washing over with gallo-nitrate of silver, and exposure to heat, would produce a similar result.

The following facts, form the substance of a paper by Mr. W. F. Channing, in a recent number of " Silliman's Journal," in which some modifications of the Calotype process are described :

In a recent process of Hunt, a paper is first prepared with iodide of silver, and then washed with ferrocyanide of potassium, and used moist. The ferrocyanide contains carbon, potassium, iron, and nitrogen without oxygen. Mixed in powder with substances abounding in oxygen, such as nitrate or chlorate of potash, it explodes by heat or percussion. In this case, it is easy to see that if water were present a slight cause would determine its oxygen to the ferrocyanide and its hydrogen to the iodine of the silver. Water in the form of water of crystallization, hygrometric moisture, or artificially applied, often thus performs an important in these preparations. The cyanide of potassium is equally or more efficacious than the ferrocyanide. Besides the inconvenience of using a moist paper, this is not so sensitive as Talbot's Calotype paper, founded on his important discovery of the properties of gallic acid.

For this the paper is washed successively with nitrate of silver and iodide of potassium; then, before using, with a mixture of acetic acid, nitrate of silver, and gallic acid, which must be made at the time. After a short exposure in the camera, the paper, still apparently unchanged, is washed again with the above mixture, when the impression begins to grow upon the paper in a very striking and beautiful manner. The objection to this process is its complication. The following is a very simple modification of it, nearly as sensitive, and more so than the original Daguerrotype plates.

A piece of best glazed letter paper is fastened by means of a penknife point and some hard wood pegs to a piece of smooth pine board. It is washed over once quickly and evenly by means of a camel-hair brush, with a solution of sixty grains crystallized nitrate of silver in one ounce of water. Let it dry spontaneously, and as soon as dry wash it for a minute with a brush and solution of ten grains of iodide of potassium in one ounce of water. Then instantly wash it with water by dipping it three or four times in a suitable vessel, and dry it by pressing it gently between blotting paper. It is then ready for the camera. One minute is sufficient for a building on which a February sun is shining; four or five minutes for general views. A rather more sensitive paper is prepared by using a mixed solution of five grains of iodide of potassium and five grains of chloride of sodium in one ounce of water, instead of the iodide of potassium. Five grains of bromide of potassium in one ounce of water form a rather less sensitive preparation. These papers may also be made more sensitive by washing them again, after the iodide of potassium, with nitrate of silver, though it will hardly repay the labour. The series of salts of silver, according to their sensibility, when afterwards brought out by gallic acid, appears to be iodide with chloride, iodide, iodide with bromide, bromide, bromide with chloride, chloride, fluoride, nitrate ; ferroycyanide, sulphocyanide, cyanide. The series with mercury differs essentially from this.

After exposure these papers are still white, but they need only to be fastened as before to another piece of board, and washed over once quickly and evenly with a saturated solution of crystallized gallic acid (only three or four grains in one ounce of water), or with solution of galls, to bring out in a few moments the hidden impression. A weak impression may be brought out by several washings, letting the paper dry between each. Too long an exposure, however, in the camera, is better than too short a one. When it has come out sufficiently, dip it in water and fix it by washing it with the iodide or other solution used in the preparation. Then wash it in water, and dry between blotting paper as before.

In views from which copies are to be taken by superposition over other sensitive paper, it is better perhaps to use the bromide throughout, as it leaves the paper whiter and more permeable to the chemical rays, or to fix the paper prepared with iodide, by washing with a bromide solution or hyposulphite of soda. Care must be taken, in making proof, not to use the nitrate of silver or galls too profusely, otherwise the paper will be stained through. Papers merely washed with nitrate of silver, used as soon as dry, and brought out afterwards by galls, may answer well for copies.

These papers should not be exposed to light or heat during any part of the process, and there should be no delay between the use of the nitrate of silver and iodide of potassium ; for the nitrate on paper is soon decomposed, so that gallic acid discolours it. The iodized paper will keep a long while, unless there is much excess of nitrate of silver. It is best, however, to use it soon after it is made.

It is important to the sensibility of all these preparations, that the nitrate of silver solution should be neutral, have no excess of acid, the electro-negative ingredient ; and also that there should be no excess of iodide of potassium, another electro-negative element, on the paper, but rather the reverse. The brushes used should be made without metal, and no metal should touch the paper during its preparation. All the parts of the operation should be kept distinct to ensure a perfect result.

The analogy in these processes to the Daguerreotype is very

interesting, iodide of silver being brought out in both cases after the action of light. Though the Daguerreotype cannot be brought out by gallic acid, yet Balard noticed a year ago that the vapour of mercury would bring out an impression on pre-pared paper. It is curious to hold one half of a piece of iodized paper, which has received an impression over mercury heated in a capsule, and wash the other half with gallic acid. The first brings out a faint positive sketch, the last a strong negative picture. By preparing a black carbonaceous paper with iodide of silver, the vapour of mercury brings out a sort of positive picture, which may deserve some attention.

The solution of galls seems to furnish much that is wanted in a secondary reducing agent. Still the field is open for inquiry. A solution of common tea, from its tannic acid, brings out an impression imperfectly well. Crenic acid, or a solution of peat, which also abstracts oxygen during its decomposition, seems also to have this property.

There is no science which is now advancing so rapidly as Photography. These processes will soon undoubtedly be superseded; they may, however, be of interest and use at the present moment.

THE CHRYSOTYPE.

The greater part of the preparations already used in Photography are of mineral origin; but latterly substances have been employed having in their constitution organic bodies, either alone, or united with a substance of a mineral nature. In the researches on the action of light on vegetable colours very recently instituted by Sir John Herschel, he found he could produce colours, such as yellow, green, blue, red, pink, and a variety of others, never before obtained by the influence of light. During the course of his experiments he found that certain salts, such as the ammonio-citrate of iron (a salt of a vegeto-mineral character), was very readily acted upon by light; but that, unless it was aided by certain metallic solutions, the effect was scarcely perceptible. When paper washed over with a solution of ammonio-citrate of iron is exposed to light for a short time with any body, such as a piece of lace, in contact with it, the part covered by the lace is left of its original colour, but the part on which the light is enabled to act becomes darker, according to the time it is exposed ; if the exposure is only of a very short duration, there is not the slightest appearance of darkening produced. It is in this state to be acted upon with a neutral solution of chloride of gold, which immediately darkens the part exposed to light, and removes the original brown colour of the ammonio-citrate from the parts to which light has had no access. In this state, however, it is still sensitive ; therefore means must be adopted to remove the sensitive compound. In order to accomplish this, it must be washed in distilled water, dried between folds of blotting-paper, and then brushed over with a solution of iodide of potassium, which must be allowed to remain on the paper for a minute or two, and then washed off with distilled water. After the picture is dry, it is no longer acted upon by light, or indeed by any substance which does not destroy the texture of the paper. The necessary solutions are prepared in the following manner :—Take 100 grains of the ammonio-citrate of iron, and dissolve them in 900 grains of distilled water. Prepare a solution of gold in nitro-hydrochloric acid (the aqua regia of the shops), taking care to perfectly neutralize any excess of acid by means of soda. The solution ought to be of such a strength as to resemble sherry wine in colour. The most convenient proportion of iodide of potassium is one ounce to the pint of distilled water.* By this process pictures exhibiting the smallest objects with perfect accuracy may be produced· This species of paper is found to be the best for taking positive copies of pictures produced by the Calotype process, as, with very little attention to the even texture of the paper, a surface may be obtained which will be free from spots, or defects of any kind.

Concluding Remarks.

The application of photography to various departments of the arts and sciences must be obvious.

The botanist, instead of employing his pencil day after day in copying the minutiæ of a plant, need only call to his aid the Calotype, and in a moment he produces a copy rivalling the original in boldness and detail. To the meteorologist this discovery will be of extreme utility, enabling him to ascertain with accuracy the amount of light falling upon a given space in a given time. Many of our scientific travellers have neither leisure

* These solutions, excepting that of iodide of potassium, ought to be kept in a dark place, and in bottles with glass stoppers.

nor ability to employ the pencil, and therefore those at a distance have to derive their only knowledge of scenery and buildings abroad from mere description. But by means of this art not only may the traveller write of the places he has seen, but he may bring home to his countrymen the graphic representation of all that has caught his attention, and this, too, by means of a camera, almost small enough to be carried in the pocket.

M. Arago, in extolling the Daguerreotype, says, "To copy the millions and millions of hieroglyphics which completely cover the great monuments of Thebes, Memphis, Carnac, &c., would require scores of years and legions of artists. With the Daguerreotype a single man would suffice to bring to a happy conclusion this vast labour. Arm the Egyptian Institution with two or three of Daguerre's instruments, and on many of the large engravings in their celebrated work, the fruit of our immortal expedition, vast assemblages of real hieroglyphics would replace fictitious or purely conventional characters. Again, these Photographic delineations having been subjected, during their formation, to the rules of geometry, shall enable us, with the aid of a few simple data, to ascertain the exact dimensions of the most elevated parts, and of edifices the most inaccessible."

In conclusion, the writer again begs to express his obligations to his valued friend, Dr. Ryan, whose exceedingly interesting lecture at the Royal Polytechnic Institution first suggested the foregoing compilation.

BOOKS

RECENTLY PUBLISHED

BY

HENRY RENSHAW, 356, STRAND.

Fourth Edition, 8vo., cloth, price 8s.,

THE ORIGINAL; consisting of Essays on whatever is most interesting and important in Religion and Politics, in Morals and Manners, and in our Habits and Customs. By the late THOMAS WALKER, M.A., Trinity College, Cambridge.

In One Volume, Illustrated, price 14s.,

THE ANATOMY OF SUICIDE. By FORBES WINSLOW, Member of the Roal College of Surgeons of London.

It is the author's object in this work to establish a fact which he believes of primary importance—viz., that the disposition to commit self-destruction is, to a great extent, amenable to those principles which regulate our treatment of ordinary diseases; and that, to a degree more than is generally supposed, it originates in physical derangement of the brain and abdominal viscera. The author has endeavoured to elucidate the state of mind which precedes the act of suicide; and to point out the relationship between these morbid feelings and certain corporeal diseases.

"The whole is arranged with great care and precision. The subject is treated in all its bearings and ramifications, and nothing appears to be left undone that can in any way illustrate and exemplify the crime. There is a vast number of very interesting anecdotes and much original matter. The treatment of the subject is, indeed, entirely original. A great mass of information is brought together with laborious industry, and rendered interesting by the demonstrative powers of the writer. Altogether the book is highly valuable."—*The Times*.

In 8vo., cloth, price 7s.,

PRACTICAL OBSERVATIONS ON DISTORTIONS OF THE SPINE, CHEST, AND LIMBS; together with Remarks on Paralytic and other Diseases connected with Impaired or Defective Motion. By WILLIAM TILLEARD WARD, F.L.S.

"This curious and interesting volume forms a striking contrast to a multitude of works on the subject of distortions, in the total absence of all quacking pretension, and in the nice application of physiological considerations, both in the discrimination of diseases apparently similar, and to the proper application of remedies."—*Athenæum*.

S. Taylor, Printer, 6, Chandos-street, Covent-garden.